U.S.A.

GALLERY BOOKS
An Imprint of W. H. Smith Publishers Inc.
112 Madison Avenue
New York City 10016

This edition first published in U.S.
in 1990 by Gallery Books,
an imprint of W.H. Smith Publishers, Inc.
112 Madison Avenue, New York, New York 10016

ISBN 0-8317-8837-2

Printed and bound in Spain

For rights information about the photographs in
this book please contact:

The Image Bank
111 Fifth Avenue, New York, N.Y. 10003

Producer: Solomon M. Skolnick
Author: Pamela Thomas
Design Concept: Leslie Ehlers
Designer: Ann-Louise Lipman
Editor: Madelyn Larsen
Production: Valerie Zars
Photo Researcher: Edward Douglas

Title page: *"Old Glory" proudly displayed for Memorial Day. The flag's 13 stripes represent the 13 original colonies; the blue field with 50 white stars represents each state in the Union.* Opposite: *Philadelphia's Independence Hall, where on July 4, 1776 the Declaration of Independence was signed.*

Describing the United States of America brings to mind the old fable of blind men trying to define an elephant. If you asked a New Englander, he would picture a varied landscape with rugged seashores, stony mountains, and pastoral valleys punctuated with old cities like Boston and Providence, rich in history and contemporary urban excitement. A Southerner would boast of broad, sandy beaches, lush pine forests, and quaint towns, while a native of Southern California would speak of palm trees, colorful deserts, movie moguls, and dusk-to-dawn nightlife.

The Assembly Room of Independence Hall was the site of the signing of the Declaration of Independence and, later, the United States Constitution. Below: Valley Forge, Pennsylvania, looks much the way it must have during the bleak winter of 1777–78, when 11,000 men were quartered here under General George Washington. Opposite: Ragged Point near Cambridge, Maryland, on the Chesapeake Bay. Once called "the Bay of the Mother of God," the Chesapeake has always been a rich source of seafood, particularly oysters and crab.

The Brandywine River near Philadelphia is at its most splendid in
autumn. Its beauty has inspired the
art of American painter Andrew
Wyeth, whose family has lived in
its valley for generations. Below:
The Inner Harbor at Baltimore,
Maryland, which is one of the largest
ports on the eastern seaboard and an
important tourist center. The Harbor
features the architecturally unique
National Aquarium.

The U.S.A. is a study in contrasts—from frigid Alaska to tropical Florida, from flat plains to high mountains, from glorious ocean beaches to tranquil lakes. Its cities are equally varied—from glamorous New York to glitzy Los Angeles. East, West, North, or South, the personality and the people of each region are shaped by their geography and history.

New England

The region known as New England, named so since virtually all who first settled there came from England, ultimately was divided into the states of Maine, New Hampshire, Vermont, Massachusetts, Rhode Island, and Connecticut. Although far wilder than any rural English county, New England's geography in many ways reflects that of Great Britain, with its rocky beaches, gnarled old mountains, soft valleys, and numerous rivers.

The U.S. Capitol building is where the United States Senate and the House of Representatives meet. The flags indicate that both houses of Congress are in session. Right: *Here the statue of Freedom atop the Capital dome. This fine example of American architecture has been "borrowed" for many state capitols.*

Today, lovely picture-book towns still dot the New England landscape from Woodstock, Vermont, to New Milford, Connecticut. Many are named for places in England—such as Sandwich, Bangor, Greenwich, and Plymouth—while others reflect names first given them by Native Americans, like Nantucket, Naugatuck, and Narragansett.

By the end of the seventeenth century Boston had emerged as the hub of New England, and it remains the largest New England city to this day. Like many American cities, Boston is sometimes rocked with urban strife, but its innate dignity and historic importance have never faded.

Mid-Atlantic Region

While the English were rushing to New England in the first years of America's development, they and others, including Dutch, German and Italian immigrants, were settling points south, areas that

This page: *The Jefferson Memorial, located at the Tidal Basin in Washington, D.C., honors Thomas Jefferson, the third President of the United States. Inside, the walls are inscribed with quotations from his writings. The statue of Abraham Lincoln, the nation's 16th President, bathed in morning light within the Lincoln Memorial. It was at this site in 1963 that Martin Luther King, Jr. gave his famous "I Have a Dream" speech.*

The White House has been the official home of the President of the United States since 1800. The elegant building is never more beautiful than in spring, when the cherry trees are in bloom. Below: *The Washington Monument, the 555-foot-high obelisk honoring the first U.S. President, defines the skyline of the nation's capital, literally—nothing may be built higher.*

would become the states of New York, New Jersey, Pennsylvania, Delaware, and Maryland. Cities like New York, Philadelphia, and Baltimore fast became major seaports and important urban centers.

New York City, said to have been bought from Native Americans and settled by the Dutch, before long became one of the nation's most ethnically diverse cities. With the Statue of Liberty graciously welcoming immigrants and visitors for over 100 years, New York has served as the front door to the United States. Despite its diversity—or perhaps because of it—New York is to the United States what London is to England or Paris is to France: the nation's City with a capital "C."

For almost two centuries, New York has been the center of business, finance, entertainment, and the arts in the United States, if not the world. Madison Avenue remains synonymous with advertising, Wall Street with finance, and Broadway with theater. New York boasts some of the world's greatest art museums and is the home office of many American businesses. Although expense, congestion, and shifting lifestyle needs are forcing changes in the "Big Apple," New York still ranks number one.

Opposite: *Some of the most famous memorials to members of the Armed Forces who died for their country. The Marine Corps Memorial, inspired by a World War II photograph of tired-yet-hopeful Marines hoisting the American flag on Mt. Suribachi, honors all Marines who died in the service of their country since the Revolution.* This page: *The Vietnam Veterans Memorial is a simple black granite structure that bears the names of the more than 58,000 Americans who died during that war. Designed by Maya Lin, its very sparseness inspires strong feelings. In Arlington National Cemetery, located across the Potomac River in Arlington, Virginia, is the final resting place of 175,000 Americans, including President John F. Kennedy and his brother, Senator Robert F. Kennedy. The Tomb of the Unknowns honors all unknown servicemen who died in the wars fought in this century.*

Opposite: *The Governor's Palace in Williamsburg, Virginia, is a faithful reconstruction of the residence used by the English governors of the Virginia Colony before the War of Independence.* This page: *The home of two Presidents. Above, George Washington's Mount Vernon is in Virginia, about 15 miles from downtown Washington. Below, Thomas Jefferson's Monticello rests on a glorious rise above Charlottesville, Virginia. The house took Jefferson 40 years to design and build, and its exquisite gardens and ingenious features reflect his taste and brilliance.*

But the mid-Atlantic corridor is peppered with cities that have been both pivotal to American history and fascinating reflections of American urban renewal. During the Colonial years, Philadelphia, "the City of Brotherly Love," held center stage, and was the site of the nation's first government. Independence Hall saw the signing of the Declaration of Independence and played host to the First Continental Congress. With its important history and its creative urban renewal, Philadelphia remains one of the nation's most vital centers.

This page: *The Parthenon in Nashville, Tennessee, a replica of the Parthenon, was built for the Tennessee Centennial in 1897, and houses the Cowan Collection of American paintings. The grave of Elvis Presley and his mansion, Graceland, are great tourist attractions in Memphis, Tennessee. The Grand Ole Opry, the most famous center for American country music and its theme park, Opryland, U.S.A., are favorites with visitors to Nashville.* Opposite: *The Wright Brothers Memorial at Kitty Hawk, North Carolina, honors Orville and Wilbur Wright, the architects of modern aviation.*

This page and opposite: *Great Smoky Mountain National Park is the largest wilderness area in the eastern United States. Shared by North Carolina and Tennessee, the Smokies support some of the country's most exotic wildlife and the most exquisite wildflowers abound.*

On the Chesapeake Bay, the centerpoint of the Eastern seaboard and a place famous for its fishing industry, sits Baltimore, Maryland. Baltimore is a unique seaport in that its hardworking people still find time for graciousness Here there is much to attract the visitor: from the first Washington Monument in its beautiful setting at Mount Vernon Place to the Inner Harbor with its shops and restaurants and the U.S. Frigate *Constellation*.

Less than 50 miles south of Baltimore is the nation's capital. Named for the first U.S. president, Washington, D.C. is not part of a state but a district—the District of Columbia. Designed by a Frenchman, Pierre L'Enfant, Washington, D.C. possesses the gleam and classic order of many European cities, yet its serenity is deceptive. Washington is not only the seat of national and world politics

Above: *Harbour Town Sea Pines is one of the loveliest areas at Hilton Head Island, South Carolina, a resort popular with families and sportsmen.* Below: *St. Phillips Church is one of many buildings—old homes, historical monuments, galleries, gardens, and churches—that make Charleston a living portrait of life in the "Old South."*

Known as "The Mt. Rushmore of the South," this monument to heroes of the Confederacy was carved into the world's largest mass of granite at Stone Mountain near Atlanta, Georgia. Below: *The entrance gate and driveway to Wormsloe, an 800-acre plantation begun in 1733 on the picturesque Isle of Hope, Savannah, Georgia.*

but sadly, bears witness to as much crime and poverty as it does style. Yet its formal buildings, such as the United States Capitol and the White House, together with a plethora of monuments, museums, libraries, and parks, make it a most treasured capital.

The Southeast

Simultaneous with the settlement of New England was the development of the American South, although,

Swan House, an Italianate antebellum home, is a short drive from downtown Atlanta. It attracts visitors with its collection of European art. Below: *Burned to the ground by General Sherman in 1864, Atlanta rebuilt itself to become the hub of the South, with the world's largest jet terminal complex.*

unlike the New England Puritans, those settling this region were intent on making money, not escaping religious strife.

The area known as Virginia originally extended from the Chesapeake Bay, across the Appalachian Mountains, to the Ohio River. Later it was cut in two, creating two states, Virginia and West Virginia. In 1607 the first permanent English settlement was established in Jamestown, Virginia. This was the beginning of the Old South, which eventually comprised the states of North Carolina, South Carolina, Georgia, Florida, Alabama, Mississippi, Tennessee, and Kentucky. Except for Kentucky, these states were among those that formed the Confederacy in 1860 and seceded from the Union, thereby igniting the Civil War.

The southern coastal regions from Norfolk, Virginia, to Savannah, Georgia, as well as the Mississippi Delta, were developed by rich landowners. Hundreds of thousands of Africans were brought to America to work the plantations.

Other states, however, such as Kentucky, Tennessee, Alabama, and Mississippi, were settled by poor farmers, most of whom remained poor.

Walt Disney World, near Orlando, Florida, is the largest recreational park in the United States. Shown here, is the Magic Kingdom. Below: *Epcot Center ("Experimental Prototype Community of Tomorrow"), located just a short monorail ride from the Walt Disney World Magic Kingdom, is another Disney dream.*

Miami, Florida, once a fading resort, is now one of America's most exciting cities. Not far from Miami's urban splendor is Everglades National Park with its exotic animals and flora like these dwarf cypress trees.

But while wealthy landowners formed the genteel, dignified culture known as the Old South, it is the combined folk knowledge of the more indigent farmers and African-Americans that is responsible for some of the most remarkable contributions to American music, fiction, and art.

For years, Louisiana's sensual and exotic New Orleans has served as the South's most important port. More French and Spanish than English, it is famous for its Cajun and Creole food, its Dixieland jazz, the incomparable joy of Bourbon Street, and the pleasures of Mardi Gras. Although New Orleans remains a much-loved city, Atlanta, Georgia, has garnered respect as the hub of the South and one of the most important cities in the entire country.

This page: *A street sign marks one of America's most famous thoroughfares. Bourbon Street is the emotional heart of New Orleans' French Quarter and is synonymous with Dixieland music, spicy Cajun food and Mardi Gras. The Cabildo, one of four buildings that make up the Louisiana State Museum, is at Jackson Square, the center of* Vieux Carré *(French Quarter). Also at Jackson Square is the St. Louis Cathedral, whose cloisters are shown here.*

The Midwest

Like the South, the American Midwest has a personality all its own. Because the Midwest covers such a vast territory—Ohio, Indiana, Illinois, Michigan, Wisconsin, Minnesota, Iowa, North Dakota, South Dakota, Nebraska, and Kansas are all considered midwestern states—it can be divided into two sections, the Great Lakes region and the Plains States.

In Hannibal, Missouri, up the river from St. Louis, is the boyhood home (and museum) of Samuel Langhorne Clemens, known to all as Mark Twain. Below: The Gateway Arch, the tallest monument (630 feet high) in the United States, stands as a tribute to St. Louis' role as the gateway to westward expansion. Designed by Eero Saarinen and completed in 1966, the arch is made of stainless steel.

The Great Lakes—Ontario, Erie, Huron, Michigan, and Superior—are the largest freshwater lakes in the world. The states that border them—Ohio, Indiana, Illinois, Michigan, Wisconsin, and Minnesota—developed primarily because of their access to the lakes. Always important waterways for transportation, the Great Lakes played a central role in the development of American industry and the growth of towns like Cleveland, Toledo, and Detroit.

Iowa, Missouri, North Dakota, South Dakota, Nebraska, Kansas, and even parts of Texas make up the Plains States, famed for undulating fields of grain and corn and massive herds of cattle. Cattle were pivotal to the development of the Great Plains, and cowboys, always considered symbols of the American West, were actually most active there. Mythic cowboy towns like Wichita and Dodge City were important forts in the state of Kansas.

Because of its futuristic architecture, Oral Roberts University, in Tulsa, Oklahoma, is sometimes referred to as "The University of Mars." But values there are old-fashioned: students cannot smoke, drink, or dance. Below: *The statue of Buffalo Bill Cody, outside the National Cowboy Hall of Fame and Western Heritage Center in Oklahoma City, captures the spirit of one of America's legendary cowboys.*

Brawny Chicago grew up because it linked the farmers and cattlemen to the rest of the country through the Great Lakes and the railways. Today, while still down-to-earth and tough, Chicago is as sophisticated as New York or Los Angeles—and certainly as important.

The Rocky Mountain States

The Rocky Mountains loom out of the Plains like a glorious monster. Spreading through Colorado, Wyoming, Montana, Idaho, and parts of Utah, they present an abrupt change from shimmering corn and wheat fields, ushering in lush pine forests and rugged, snow-capped peaks.

Above: A fragment of petrified wood photographed at Petrified Forest National Park. About 100 miles east of Flagstaff, Arizona, the park also includes the famous Painted Desert. Below: A distinctive church at the Taos, New Mexico, Indian pueblo. Taos was settled by Spaniards in the early 17th century, who no doubt were as enchanted by its physical radiance then as artists are now. Overleaf: These surrealistic buttes, set against a melancholic sky, provide just a hint of the awesome natural scenery in the Southwest.

Opposite: Built by the Spanish early in the 18th century, the Alamo in San Antonio, Texas, was the site of a heroic defense by Americans during Texas' battle for independence in 1836. The skyline of Dallas changes weekly, according to some residents. Here at sunset the glass towers are particularly striking.

Although the Rocky Mountain states cover a large portion of the country's total landmass, they are home to only five percent of its population. A fair amount of the land is preserved for national parks, such as Yellowstone, Grand Teton, and Mesa Verde.

Although farming is still the primary industry of the Rocky mountain region, the area is more famous for its glorious skiing at such resorts as Sun Valley, Idaho, and Aspen, Colorado. Denver is the only city of any size in the region, yet it is not really part of the West, but the last stop on the Great Plains.

The Southwest

Some people swear that there is no land more beautiful than the American Southwest. New Mexico, Arizona, and Nevada are the states most commonly associated with the region, but Utah shares some of their scenic wonders, which include

This page: *Montezuma's Castle, a five-story, 20-room adobe cliff-dwelling near Flagstaff, Arizona. It was built about A.D. 1100 by the Sinagua Indians. Antelope House, a 12th-century adobe remnant of the Anasazi civilization, is one of many remarkable sights at Canyon de Chelly National Monument.*
Opposite: *The distinctive buttes of the Grand Canyon, the nation's most famous natural wonder.*

Denver, Colorado, nicknamed "the Mile-High City," was founded in 1858.
Opposite: Sievers Mountain, a splendid ridge of snow-capped peaks, explains
why Aspen has become one of America's most popular ski resorts.

the Grand Canyon and Canyon de Chelley in Arizona, the Carlsbad Caverns in New Mexico, and Zion National Park in Utah. Wondrous expanses of desert also characterize all parts of the Southwest.

The population of this region is as distinctive and beautiful as the scenery. Mexican-Americans, Native Americans, and "Anglos" share a turbulent history yet have found a common ground, and today they live together in tranquility and mutual respect.

Above: *This snowy-looking expanse is the Bonneville Salt Flats, part of the Great Salt Lake Desert in Utah.* Below: *The angel Moroni stands atop the highest tower of the Mormon Temple and watches over Temple Square in Salt Lake City, Utah, the headquarters of the 3-million-member Church of Jesus Christ of Latter-day Saints.*

Above: *The neon marquee of The Golden Nugget, one of Las Vegas, Nevada's most renowned casinos. In Arches National Park, Utah, ancient red sandstone has been eroded by water and wind, leaving fantastic spires, pinnacles, and over 200 remarkable arches. Pictured here is one of the famed "Windows."*

Above: *These Indian kilns are among the few manmade sights in Death Valley, California. Death Valley, in the Mojave Desert, is often thought to be an arid wasteland, and yet its wildflowers, colored canyon walls, and salt lakes make it one of the country's great natural wonders.* Below: *Hearst Castle, the fascinating, opulent home of newspaper magnate William Randolph Hearst, stands near San Simeon, California*

Right: Mickey Mouse leads a parade of Disney characters at Disneyland in Anaheim, California. Built in 1955, Disneyland is known through-out the world as the U.S.A.'s most astonishing recreational park. Below: The Sleeping Beauty Castle in Disneyland beckons visitors to cross the moat into Fantasyland.

Most of the cities of the Southwest—such as Sante Fe, Phoenix, and Tucson—are refined, relaxed, easy-going centers, offering a pleasant lifestyle infused with artistic predilections. The only exception is Las Vegas, Nevada, a gaudy, "bad-girl" town, loved for her casinos and her hilarious vulgarity.

California

Although California is just one state, it is more like two separate nations. Southern California, home of the perennial suntan, epitomizes twentieth-century American life. San Diego, with its perfect climate and exquisite suburban towns, has been called "America's Finest City," but it is Los Angeles that symbolizes the nation's present and future.

This page: *The famous "Hollywood" sign, with its 50-foot-high letters, was once an advertisement for a subdivision in the Hollywood Hills. It now stands not only for a city but also for a fascinating segment of American culture. Los Angeles at evening, photographed from one of the high ridges that surround the city, is a sight* Angelenos *and others love. Opposite: Unlike sun-worshipping, flashy Los Angeles, San Francisco has dignity and ethereal elegance.*

Known for its smog, ubiquitous freeways, automobiles, Hollywood glitz, and hard-boiled natives, Los Angeles is a multifaceted sprawl that incorporates everything from sedate Pasadena to glamorous Beverly Hills. Disneyland, the country's most famous tourist attraction, lies just to the south, and California's exquisite coastline drifts lazily to the north.

San Francisco is the jeweled heart of Northern California, a dignified lady on the bay, where a gentle fog replaces smog and handsome streets pay homage to the city's history rather than the nation's future. Further north

Opposite: The Golden Gate Bridge, one of the most famous bridges in the world, spans the Golden Gate strait that separates the Pacific Ocean from San Francisco Bay. This page: Charming Victorian houses, trimmed with delectable "gingerbread" and painted in candy-mint colors, give San Francisco much of its charm. Cable cars, declared a national historic landmark in 1964, provide a unique and certainly memorable mode of transportation for viewing San Francisco. Turning them around just looks complicated.

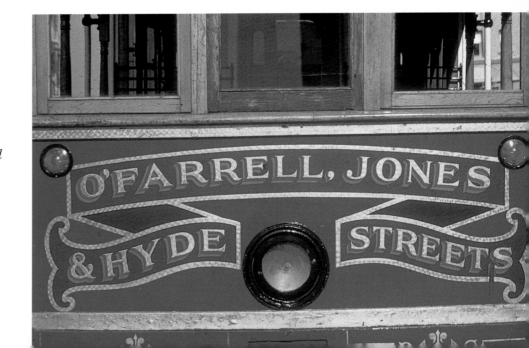

Above: *Tufa formations, formed by calcareous and siliceous rock deposits, make Mono Lake appear to be a lunar landscape rather than what one normally associates with California. Below: Bixby Bridge, Big Sur, possibly the most majestic stretch along California's central coast.*

Above: *Lone cypress, one of the most photographed of the rare Monterey cypresses.* Below: *The Marin headlands, just west of San Francisco's Golden Gate Bridge. Overleaf: Yosemite National Park, one of California's most popular tourist attractions.*

in California lie the redwoods,
the Napa Valley (known for its
world-class wines), and more
handsome scenery where the
legacies of cowboys, Spanish
monks, trappers, and gold-
rushers are still in evidence.

The Pacific Northwest

Settled late in the nineteenth
century by Americans still
questing for the last frontier,
the Pacific Northwest, which
includes the states of Washington and Oregon, boasts
some of the most awesome and
grand scenery in the United
States. Despite the relative
sophistication of its two major
cities, Seattle and Portland,
the Pacific Northwest is really
for those who love the outdoors.

This page: *Crater Lake, in Oregon's
Crater Lake National Park, sits high
up in the mountains. The lake is an
almost perfect circle, with Wizard
Island forming a tiny peak in its
center. A snow-capped Mt. Hood
provides a handsome backdrop for
Portland, one of Oregon's most cos-
mopolitan cities. The Space Needle
offers an interesting juxtaposition
to the sedate skyline of Seattle,
Washington. Opposite: The North
Cascade Mountains in Washington
State are relatively young, geolog-
ically speaking. Beautiful Mt. Baker
has been erupting frequently since
1974.*

Above: *Mt. St. Helens, notorious for its devastating volcanic eruption in 1980, appears very tranquil now.* Below: *Mt. McKinley National Park, a 3,000-square-mile area north of Anchorage, is named for the U.S.'s highest mountain, known also by its Indian name, Denali.*

Above: *"Sea stacks" are formations unique to the Pacific Northwest coastline. These were photographed off La Push, Washington.* Below: *Because of Alaska's proximity to the Arctic Circle, the sun lights the sky 20 hours a day in midsummer.*

With its exquisite coastline, magnificent forests and mountain ranges, it is a wild-and-woolly countryside, tamed only slightly in recent years into one of the country's most vital regions.

Alaska and Hawaii

Alaska and Hawaii were not only the last two states to enter the Union (both in 1959), they also are the only two states not part of the contiguous forty-eight. Alaska lies north of Canada's British Columbia while Hawaii sits, gemlike, in the middle of the Pacific Ocean.

Opposite: *One of the constantly erupting volcanos that contribute to the awesome beauty of the Hawaiian Islands. The City of Refuge, an evocative remnant of the ancient Polynesian culture that flourished in the islands.* This page: *The U.S.S. Arizona National Memorial was built over the sunken hull of the ship that entombs the more than 1,000 sailors who died when the Japanese bombed Pearl Harbor on December 7, 1941.* Below: *A timeless Hawaiian landscape.*

Opposite: *Old Faithful, the legendary geyser that erupts every 45 to 70 minutes, is the main attraction of its kind at Wyoming's Yellowstone National Park. The park has over 10,000 other geysers.* This page: *A night sky over Minneapolis, Minnesota. The "Twin Cities" of Minneapolis and St. Paul are home to large corporations, great museums and impressive historic neighborhoods. Mt. Rushmore National Monument, in the Black Hills of South Dakota, was begun by sculptor Gutzon Borglum in 1923 and completed in 1941. Presidents Washington, Jefferson, Lincoln and Theodore Roosevelt are represented.*

Above: *Farms such as this are found throughout Wisconsin, "America's Dairyland." *Below: *Long a city of skyscrapers, Chicago is the hub of the Midwest and the nation's third- largest city. *Opposite: *Built in 1867, the Chicago Water Tower and Pumping Station still supply water to the Near North Side. They are among the few structures to survive the Great Fire of 1871.*

Above: *Detroit's soaring Renaissance Center (Ren Cen) hosts many conventions and is an excellent example of modern American architecture.*
Below: *One of the most stunning waterfalls in the world, Niagara Falls figured prominently in Native American legends and in 19th-century art. Later it became the "Honeymoon Capital of the World" and attracts over 10 million visitors a year.*

The sea and New England are synonomous as these pictures show. Top to bottom: This lighthouse at Cape Elizabeth is typical of many that dot the jagged coast of Maine. Lobstering has always been an important industry in the state, and lobster pots such as these in West Tremont are a common sight. This red fisherman's shack in Rockport on Cape Ann, Massachusetts, is such a favorite subject of artists and photographers that the town voted to have it rebuilt when it was destroyed in a hurricane several years ago.

Bought in 1867 for two cents an acre, Alaska was originally known as Seward's Folly, so called because Secretary of State William Seward was responsible for its purchase. By the end of the nineteenth century, however, enough gold had been found to turn a billion-dollar profit, thus restoring Seward's reputation.

While Alaska is the largest state in the Union (586,400 square miles), it is the smallest in population, with most inhabitants living in the cities of Anchorage and Juneau. Most of the land is designated as National Preserve and is rich not only in gold but also in some of the nation's most exciting scenery and in all manner of wildlife, from Kodiak bears to bald eagles.

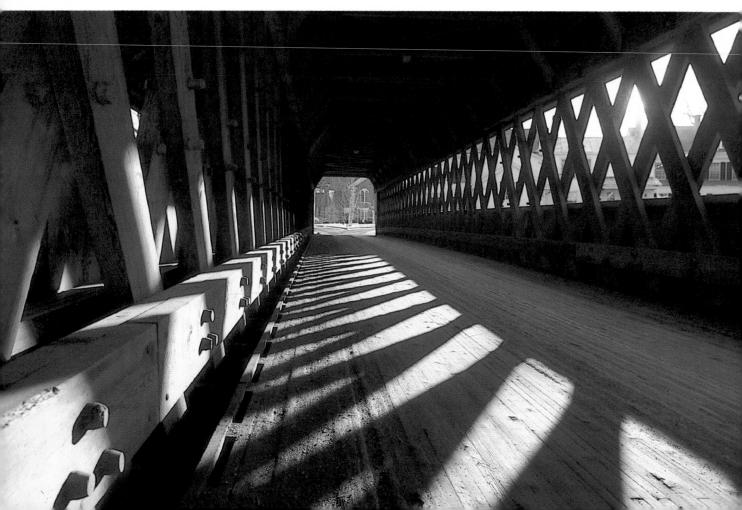

The state of Hawaii is made up of eight islands, with the capital city of Honolulu located on the large island of Oahu. Originally the ancestral home of the Polynesians, Hawaii now is a mélange of various Oriental and Occidental cultures.

Tourists by the tens of thousands flock to Hawaii every year, the tourist trade, after the sugar cane industry, being the state's greatest source of income. It is truly a tropical paradise, replete with smoldering volcanos, exotic fruits and flowers, and some of the most inviting beaches in the world.

The words and pictures in this book can do no more than offer a glimpse of a vast country that Nature has endowed with great physical beauty and that America's people have enriched by their labor and creativity. The United States itself will do the rest.

Opposite: Quintessential Vermont. A simple, white church set amid fall foliage and a beautiful covered bridge; this one is in Woodstock. This page: Quintessential Boston: The spire of Old North Church and a statue of Paul Revere, the man who made the church and himself part of American legend. Old North Bridge, at nearby Concord, also figured in the Revolution. Sculling on the Charles, the river that separates Boston and Cambridge.

Opposite: *Once a year the U.S.S Constitution, "Old Ironsides," a 44-gun frigate that saw action during the War of 1812, is taken out from the Navy Yard at Charlestown to be turned around so that her hull will weather evenly.* This page: *The lower Manhattan skyline as photographed from the Staten Island ferry. At 25 cents round trip, the ride is the best buy in New York. The Twin Towers of the World Trade Center, now the tallest buildings in New York City, "flank" the Statue of Liberty, but only in this photograph.*

Above: *Designed by Frederick Law Olmsted and Calvert Vaux in the 1860's, Central Park was one of the first land-scaped urban parks in the United States. Today, its 800-acres are a year-round delight to millions of New Yorkers. Built in 1883, the Brooklyn Bridge, which connects lower Manhattan to Brooklyn, was then considered one of the greatest engineering feats of the 19th century. Today, it has become one of the most photographed bridges in the world.*
Opposite: *The Chrysler Building and the Empire State Building, two superb examples of Art Deco architecture, may no longer be the tallest skyscrapers in the world, but they still epitomize New York.*

INDEX OF PHOTOGRAPHY